YOUTH FICTION

Ryan Sees *Red*

Peter Leigh

Published in association with
The Basic Skills Agency

Hodder & Stoughton

Orders: please contact Bookpoint Ltd, 39 Milton Park, Abingdon, Oxon OX14
4TD. Telephone: (44) 01235 400414, Fax: (44) 1235 400454.
Lines are open from 9.00-6.00, Monday to Saturday, with a 24 hour message
answering service. Email address: orders@bookpoint.co.uk

British Library Cataloguing in Publication Data
A catalogue record for this title is available from The British Library

ISBN 0 340 69698 2

First published 1997
Impression number   10 9 8 7 6 5 4 3 2
Year   2004 2003 2002 2001 2000 1999 1998

Copyright © 1997 Peter Leigh

Typeset by Fakenham Photosetting Ltd, Fakenham, Norfolk.
Printed in Great Britain for Hodder & Stoughton Educational,
a division of Hodder Headline Plc, 338 Euston Road, London NW1 3BH
by Athenæum Press Ltd, Gateshead, Tyne & Wear.

Ryan Sees Red

Contents

1

Sophie 4 Ryan

There were two things in Ryan's life.

Football and girls.

And he was good at both!

He was tall and fit,

and played football well.

But it wasn't just that he played well.

He made the others play well too.

He had an open, easy-going way about him.

This made the others like him and respect him.

'Right lads,' he would say, clapping his hands.
'Let's have another go.'
And the whole team would try harder.
For Ryan.
Because he had asked them.

'That Ryan,' people said.
'He'll go far.'

When he was talking to a girl,
he had the same easy way.
She would lean back,
and run her hand through her hair,
and flash her eyes at him.
And Ryan would smile his easy, open smile,
and she would find herself talking more,
and laughing more.

He wasn't like other boys.

He didn't try to impress her with

how strong he was, or how hard he was.

He didn't have to.

He seemed to really like her as a person,

and this made her really like him.

'That Ryan,' people said.

'It'll be a lucky girl who gets him.'

But no girl ever did,

although all the girls in school tried.

Ryan would go out with them once or twice,

but no more.

He was always with one girl or another,

but it never led to anything.

They didn't mind,

because Ryan was nice and fun to be with,

and didn't boast or lie about it afterwards

like other boys.

And also they didn't mind
because they knew about Sophie!
Sophie was the one girl in the school
who hadn't been out with Ryan,
and who didn't want to go out with him.
And of course, she was the one girl
who Ryan did want to go out with.

He had wanted to go out with her
ever since the first day at school,
when he had sat behind her.
She had leant forward to write her name
on her book.
Ryan had seen the soft curve of her neck
as her hair fell over her face.
He felt his insides lurch.
He looked over her shoulder,
and saw her write 'Sophie'.

'Sophie', he said to himself,

as if it was the best name in the world,

'Sophie'.

And then inside his pencil case he wrote

'Sophie 4 Ryan'.

But Sophie never wrote 'Ryan 4 Sophie'.

She would not go out with him

even though he asked her and asked her.

Even though he kept putting

little presents in her desk.

Ryan never told anyone else about Sophie,

but all the girls knew,

the way girls do know about these things.

'Go on, Sophie,' the other girls would say.

'Why don't you go out with him?

He's lovely.'

But Sophie just hid behind her hair,

and said nothing.

2

Dreams

Ryan was the captain of a local team.

This season was their best one ever.

They stood a good chance of winning
the city cup.

But they had to win their next match
on Saturday.

If they won, they would be in the final.

They were playing a team from the other side
of the city.

The coach gathered the team around him

in the changing-room before the match.

'Right lads,' he said.

'I've been speaking to the other coach.

Half his team are injured,

and the other half are ill.

They've had to scrape the barrel

just to get eleven players.

But don't get too sure of yourselves.

The game's not won yet!

I want one hundred per cent

from each one of you.'

Ryan nodded and grinned.

This was going to be easy!

He could feel his fingers

around the cup already.

It was as good as won.

Sometimes people from the big clubs

in London came to see the final.

Perhaps Spurs or Arsenal would see him,

and sign him.

He could see himself now holding the cup,

with the crowd cheering and Sophie

looking up at him.

'Oh Ryan,' she would say, 'Oh Ryan!'

He brought himself back down to earth.

First they had to beat this other lot.

He ran out on to the pitch.

The others won the toss.

The teams lined up, and the striker from the

other side stepped forward to take the kick-off.

There was a gasp from Ryan's team!

The striker was a girl!

It was Sophie!

3

The Big Game

All the team stared at her.

The referee was just going to blow the whistle,

when the coach came running on.

'Stop the game!' he shouted.

'Stop the game! That's a girl!'

'So what?' said the referee.

'We can't play against girls!'

'Why not?

There's nothing in the rules against it.'

'But that's crazy.

They might get hurt.

They might... they might...'

The coach couldn't think of words to say.

The other coach came running on,

and there was a big argument between them

and the referee in the middle of the pitch.

The players waited quietly.

Finally it was settled.

Ryan's coach turned to his team and said,

'Right lads.

It seems there's nothing we can do about it.

They haven't got anyone else,

and she only agreed to play at the last minute.

So you've just got to forget she's a girl,

and play your normal game. OK?'

'OK, boss!' said the team,

and ran back to their positions ready to play.

Except Ryan!

Forget she's a girl?

Play your normal game?

Impossible!

It was Sophie!

His Sophie!

He had heard of girl footballers of course.

Some of them played in other local clubs.

Some of them were really good,

so he had heard.

But he had never actually played against one!

And never, never, had he thought

he would ever play against Sophie!

It was just impossible!

Unthinkable!

But here she was.
The impossible was happening!

The whistle blew,
and Sophie kicked off.

Ryan was confused.
He couldn't see straight.
His insides had lurched the moment
he had seen Sophie,
just like that first day at school.
And now he felt as if he couldn't move.
He had to force himself to run,
but it was like wading through mud.
He shook his head to try and focus,
but it was no good.
It was like a dream.

A bad dream!

It wasn't just that Sophie was there.
It was that she was good!
She was very good!

She had a natural feel for the game,
and an easy grace
that made the boys look heavy and slow.
She was always in exactly the right place
at exactly the right time.
She had lovely ball control,
and her passes were always quick and sharp.

'Come on, Ryan!
Wake your ideas up!'

It was the coach's voice from the side.
The game was going on around him.

The other side were attacking.

And then suddenly Sophie was in front of him

with the ball at her feet.

Everything seemed in slow motion.

Ryan could only watch as those long, slim legs

moved first one way, then the other,

and then slipped by him.

He turned and saw Sophie steady herself,

and kick the ball hard.

It curved in a beautiful arc into

the top corner of the net.

One-nil!

Her team crowded round Sophie,

hugging her and clapping her on the back.

'Brilliant!' they said.

'Great!'

Ryan's team gathered around him.

'Get a grip, Ryan,' they said.

'She's only a girl.'

Ryan tried to pull himself together.

He tried to concentrate.

But the other team now knew Sophie could

beat him, and passed to her more and more.

And each time she had the ball,

Sophie ran past him on one side or the other,

making him look more and more stupid.

And with Ryan playing badly,

the whole team played badly.

Somehow they kept going to half time.

The coach was angry.

'What do you think you're doing, Ryan,

letting a girl run round you like that?

Pull yourself together.'

He's right, thought Ryan.

I mustn't let myself be beaten by a girl.

She's only a girl, even if she is Sophie.

I can't be beaten by a girl.

I won't be beaten by a girl.

He felt himself getting angrier and angrier.

He clenched his fists,

and gritted his teeth.

'She won't get past me!' he hissed.

'She won't get past me!'

4

Sent Off!

The second half started slowly.

Ryan's team started to get itself together.

Then the ball was passed to Sophie.

This is it, thought Ryan,

I'll get her now.

He ran up to her fiercely,

and lunged his foot out at the ball.

Sophie shifted a little to one side.

She held the ball at her feet,

pulled it to one side,

and then tapped it between his legs.

She skipped past him,

gathered the ball behind him,

and shot it low into the corner of the net.

Two-nil!

Ryan stood like a statue,

staring at the ground.

The ball had gone between his legs!

Between his legs!!!

The worst mistake any player could make!

The game restarted.

'Ryan. Wake up!'

screamed the coach.

Ryan looked up.

He was still in a dream.

He saw Sophie running gracefully towards the
goal with the ball at her feet.

Sophie!

His Sophie!

She had made him look a fool.

She had made him look stupid

in front of his team,

in front of his coach,

in front of everybody.

And after everything he had done for her!

All those presents he had given her!

And now she had ruined everything.

She had ruined his team,

ruined his chances with Spurs or Arsenal,

and she had ruined his love.

A wild anger gripped him.

He wanted to hurt her!

He rushed at her from behind,

and charged into her.

And at the same time he took her legs

from under her with a vicious, angry kick.

Sophie cried out,

and crashed to the ground.

The referee blew his whistle,

and pointed to the penalty spot.

Then he walked over to Ryan,

and pulled out the red card!

Ryan didn't say anything.

He didn't look at anyone.

He just walked off slowly.

Behind him Sophie was helped to her feet.

The trainer sprayed her ankle to ease the pain.

She said she was OK.

She placed the ball,

and took the penalty.

She scored!

Three-nil!

And a hat trick for Sophie!

Ryan heard the cheers in the changing-room.

He didn't have a shower or anything.

He just threw his stuff into a bag,

and walked out.

He went out of the ground,

and started to walk home.

He didn't want to see the rest of the team

or the coach.

He just wanted to be by himself.

But at the last moment he changed his mind.

There was a little park by the entrance

to the ground with some trees and bushes.

Ryan ran into these and hid.

Then he waited!

5

Shame

Sophie felt great!

Apart from her ankle.

They had won three-nil,

and she had scored a hat trick.

She was voted the best player.

The coach of Ryan's team came over to

congratulate her.

'I've never seen anything like it,' he said.

'Where did you learn to play like that?'

'Well,' said Sophie.
'I've got three brothers,
and if you have three brothers,
you have to like football.
But they play in another league out of town,
so I've only played there.'

'What do your friends at school think?'

'I haven't told them I play football.'
She hadn't told them
because she thought they would laugh at her.

'And are you going to carry on?'

'No, I don't think so. I only played today
because the team was so short.

I enjoyed it,

but I wouldn't want to play every Saturday.

I like playing just for fun.

This is too serious.'

She winced as she said this.

She could feel the pain in her ankle.

'Yes,' said the coach.

'I'm sorry about that.

I don't know what came over Ryan.

He's not normally like that.'

Sophie smiled, but said nothing.

She was a bit worried about Ryan.

What was he going to do?

What would he say to her?

She got changed,

and then said goodbye to everyone,

and thanked them for the game.

They gave her a big cheer,

and the sound of it was still in her ears

as she walked out of the ground,

and started home.

She was limping a little from her ankle.

And suddenly there in front of her was Ryan.

6

Making Up

He was still in his football kit.

She could see he was angry and hurt.

'Why did you do that to me?'

'Do what to you?'

'Make me look stupid!'

'What do you mean?

I didn't make you look stupid.
It was just a game.'

'Just a game?

You made me look stupid in front of

everybody.

You did it on purpose!'

'Of course I didn't!'

'Yes, you did!

You were trying to show me up!

And after everything I've done for you.'

'What?

What do you mean?

What have you done for me?'

'All the presents I gave you.'

'Presents?

But nobody asked you.

You just...'

'I liked you!

You knew I liked you!

You were my Sophie!'

'Your Sophie?'

'Yes! How could you do it to me?'

'I do it to you?'

By now Sophie was angry too.

'Wait a minute!

What about what you did to me?

You nearly broke my leg.

I can hardly walk.'

'Well, what do you expect,

showing off like that?'

'Showing off?'

'Yes! Showing off your legs in front
of all the boys.'

'What?'

'That's why you did it, isn't it?
You just wanted all the boys to look at you.
Girls playing football! It's disgusting!
It shouldn't be allowed. You're just a...'

'I'm not listening to this!' Sophie turned,
and tried to walk away,
but Ryan grabbed her shoulder.

'Let go of me!'
She tried to twist away.
'You hear me,' shouted Ryan.
'You're disgusting!
You're just a...'

Sophie swung round to face him.

'You're jealous, that's all!'

'What?'

Ryan let go as if he had been stung.

'Yes! Jealous! That's it!'

Sophie could feel the tears coming,

but she fought them down.

'You're jealous because you were beaten.

Beaten by me.

I'm a better player than you!'

'What? Better?

Better than me?'

'Yes! Better!

Everyone thinks you're so sweet and so lovely,

but underneath you're like all the other boys!

Your Sophie!

You think girls are there just for you.

Well, I'm not your Sophie.

You don't own me, Ryan!'

'Why!... you... you!'

Ryan grabbed her again.

He had lost control.

She had smashed his hopes, his dreams,

his everything. He shook her.

'Let me go!' she shouted.

'Let me go!'

And then Sophie's ankle gave way.

'Oh!' she cried, and fell to the ground.

Ryan stood over her,

his face twisted and his fists clenched.

There on the ground in front of him was

Sophie. His Sophie.

She was holding her ankle,

and crying out in pain.

He had done this to her!

He, Ryan!

He had kicked the ankle from under her!

And had been sent off! Sent off!

The shame welled up in Ryan,

together with all his pain, and all his hurt,

and all his feelings for Sophie.

And he broke down.

There by the side of the road

for the first time ever,

in front of Sophie, a girl,

he burst into tears.

He sunk to his knees,

and covered his face with his hands,

and sobbed.

Sophie looked at him.

The throbbing in her ankle started to go down.

'Oh Ryan,' she said at last.

And then, very gently, she reached out,

and put her arms round him.

7

Winning

They were sitting on a park bench.

Ryan had stopped crying.

'I'm sorry,' he said at last.

'What for?'

'Your ankle...'

'It's all right. It'll mend.'

'... and for crying.'

'For crying?'

'Yes. For going all soft, and crying.'

Sophie smiled at him.
'If more boys cried like that,
the world would be a happier place.'

'It's just that things got too much for me.'

'Things do.
For everybody.
And then the best thing to do is to cry.
It lets it all out.'

'I never knew you could play football.'

'There's a lot you don't know.
You never asked.
Boys always think they know everything.'
Her voice was mocking but gentle.

'And Sophie, you were good.
Really good. I mean that.'

Sophie looked pleased.
'Thank you,' she said.

'That first goal was brilliant,
the way you slipped past me.
And the second was even better.'
There was a pause.
Sophie smiled happily.

'You were a bit lucky in the third, though.'

'What? Lucky?
I was not lucky. I was...'
Sophie swung round angrily.
Ryan was grinning at her.
'Oh, you!' she said laughing.

'Are you going to carry on playing?'
said Ryan. 'You should do.
You could do really well.'

'Don't you start.
I like football, but not that much.
Besides, I'd get hacked to pieces
by boys like you.
What about you?
Will you be suspended?
Will they let you play again?'

She sounded concerned.

'Oh yes! I'll get a telling off,
but that's all.
I've never been sent off before.
And we're out of the cup,
but we've still got the league.
We'll pick ourselves up.'

He looked closely at Sophie.

'If you don't want to play football,
what do you want to do?'

'Oh, all sorts of things.
I've got all sorts of dreams.
But right now, what I really want to do
is go home and have a good rest.'
She got up, and made ready to go.

'I know something else you really want to do!'

'What? What do you mean?
What do I really want to do?'

'What you really want to do is...'
Ryan paused, and looked straight at her.
'Yes?'
'Go out with me tonight!'
'Why, Ryan! You've got a cheek!'

His eyes were still on her.
She blushed a little.

'You've got to let me show I'm sorry!'
'I don't know...'

He was all muddy,

and there were tear stains on his cheeks,

but through it all she could see that open,

easy Ryan smile.

'... well, maybe...'

The smile widened.

'... oh, all right!'